Porsche 924 & 944

Ian Wagstaff

CLASSICS IN COLOUR

Porsche 924 & 944

COLOUR, DATA AND DETAIL ON THE FOUR-CYLINDER FRONT-ENGINED CARS INCLUDING 968

Nigel Edwards

Windrow & Greene Automotive

Published in Great Britain by
Windrow & Greene Ltd
5 Gerrard Street
London W1V 7LJ

British Library Cataloguing in Publication Data
Edwards, Nigel
    Porsche 924 & 944. — (Classics in colour)
    I. Title   II. Series
    629.2222

ISBN 1 87200 476 8

Book Design: *ghk* DESIGN, Chiswick, London

Printed in Hong Kong; Bookbuilders Ltd

Contents

Porsche Cars GB

Porsche Cars GB

Acknowledgements

With this as with any book, there have been more people than just the author involved. I would particularly like to thank Simon Painter, my near neighbour and professional photographer, who took nearly all the pictures (those that are not his are credited) and painstakingly developed them to ensure the best possible results. Most of the photographs were taken on my own property, in Somerset. However, my thanks also go to Hugh Sexey's Middle School and John Schroeder of the Sexey's Arms, both at Blackford, Somerset, and Steve and Midge Garge of Stoughton, Somerset, for kind permission to use their premises for some photographic sessions.

Many of the cars illustrated belong to Porsche Club Great Britain members. Their co-operation is greatly appreciated, especially those who drove many miles to keep appointments with myself and my photographer.

Claire Knee of Porsche Cars Great Britain and Roy Gillham and Veronique at Porsche Club Great Britain's headquarters all supplied help and information, as did Clive Househam, editor of 911 & Porsche World magazine.

My thanks to Windrow & Greene's editorial director, Bryan Kennedy, for his support and suggestions during the preparation of the book. And, finally, thanks to my wife, Jean, and daughter, Charlotte, for help and encouragement throughout.

Nigel Edwards
Wedmore, Somerset, November 1991

Introduction

Mention the word 'Porsche' and the vast majority of people will think immediately of the 911, the rear-engined air-cooled classic which has been in production since 1964.

Yet its front-engined water-cooled stablemate, the Porsche 924, has been around for quite some time, too: since November 1975, in fact. And its aggressive-looking companion, the 944, made its debut a full decade ago, in the autumn of 1981.

The 924 and 944 models have enjoyed considerable success, rewarding both to their manufacturer and their many thousands of owners. Yet it was by no means a predictable success; nor was it a case of unanimous applause at first sight, although many of the initial doubts and criticisms of the cars were eventually dispelled. In the light of subsequent developments, the introduction of the 924 was the right move at the right time.

The oil crisis of 1973-74 had brought about a great deal of serious rethinking in the automobile industry. Volkswagen was planning to replace its mid-engined VW-Porsche 914 with a more conventional

Arrival of the 924 brought mixed reactions, but the range was to undergo many refinements throughout its life.

Porsche Cars GB

It won't be the price that takes your breath away.

£9403. A lot for a car, very little for a Porsche.
The 924. A 2+2 coupé built to many traditional Porsche principles. 12,000 mile service intervals. Unique 6 year Long-life warranty certifying reliability, light responsive steering and ever-pleasing Porsche performance.

And establishing a few new Porsche principles of its own.

For example, the front-mounted engine and rear-mounted transmission connected by a rigid central tube. A layout shared by the £22,000 Porsche 928.

Quite simply, this transaxle arrangement means you can drive quicker, safer. Take bends faster. Hold your own in crosswinds. Brake straighter and offer better protection to you and your passengers.

When we build the 924 we weld the parts, finish the paintwork and stitch the upholstery by hand.

We also incorporate the same fuel injection, twist and five-speed gear pattern as in the famed Porsche 911SC.

When you drive it you'll have a top speed in excess of 125mph.*
When you run it like Autocar you'd get over 25mpg* and overall running costs per mile below those of a Mini.*

And, when you resell it, there's an expensive 13 cu ft luggage space, accessible through the counter-balanced tailgate.

Initially we suggested the price wouldn't take your breath away.
On second thoughts it might.

PORSCHE 924
56 FILES 66

Photos Porsche Cars GB

**FORGED IN THE
HEAT OF COMPETITION.
THE NEW 944 TURBO.**

Developed originally for the Porsche Turbo Cup, one of Europe's most hotly contested race series, it now graduates to the road. With honours.

Racing is in its blood. But more importantly racing technology is in its engine.

The 2.5 litre power unit, already hailed as "the world's best fully crystallised" is now goes a larger turbo charger, raised boost pressure and revised engine Management System.

This lifts output to 250bhp. And makes the 944 turbo one of the few cars in the world to reach the elusive 100bhp per litre mark. In Porsche's case, underlining performance but not undermining reliability.

Stiffer suspension on the track has also produced firmer suspension for the road. Handling becomes even more precise and responsive.

Roadholding is also enhanced. The 944 Turbo now runs on ultra-wide forged alloy wheels shod with ultra-low profile tyres.

While for extra traction, there's another attraction. A limited slip differential is now standard.

Stopping power? Prodigious. To halt a machine capable of reaching 60 in 5.3 seconds and taking the chequered flag at 161mph, 4 piston fixed calliper discs and race-digital-engin-ics ABS are taken directly from the Turbo Cup.

The Press were impressed.

MOTOR SPORT: The 944 Turbo "has almost unrivalled overtaking powers ... braking performance is superb."

PERFORMANCE CAR: It proves "that 4 cylinders can do everything that 5, 6, even 12 can achieve."

AUTOCAR & MOTOR: "devastatingly quick" the 944 Turbo "has such tremendous grip ... it seems to defy the very laws of physics."

To confirm these views from the driver's seat, contact your nearest Official Porsche Centre. Or call 0734 323 459.

Then you'll discover the one thing that the 944 Turbo doesn't have on the road. Competition.

PORSCHE
BUILDING ON ACHIEVEMENT

Top: The 924 was intended as the affordable Porsche which would take the company into a much wider market. Cheap in relation to other Porsches, it was still in many people's eyes an expensive piece of machinery.
Above: Motorsport has always been an essential component of Porsche research and development. Also a valuable publicity aid, as evidenced by this 944 Turbo advertisement.

front-engined sports car and had asked Porsche to develop such a model. By early 1975, however, when prototypes were already being tested, new leadership at VW resulted in a change of course and the project was axed. Porsche immediately saw its chance. For some time, it had been felt that the company was highly vulnerable, with only the 911 model in its 'range'. Senior management were keen to introduce a cheaper and higher-volume sports car, which would make ownership of a Porsche available to a far greater public. When VW sold the design back to Porsche in the spring of 1975, the first 'entry level' Porsche, the 924, was born. To have the first production models rolling off the line at VW's plant at Neckarsulm later in the same year was a considerable achievement.

Just as when the 911 first appeared, there were many who did not accept the 924 as a 'real' Porsche. The 911's engine had six cylinders and this had proved unacceptable to diehard owners of its famous precursor, the 356, which had four cylinders — just like the 924. In fact, the 924 engine came from the Audi 100 (and the VW LT van in carburetted form), but with K-Jetronic fuel injection developing 125bhp. This again incurred the displeasure of diehard Porsche enthusiasts, to whom the picking-and-mixing of components from more prosaic vehicles resulted in what they disparaged as a 'Porsche kit car' — a betrayal, in many people's eyes, of all that the company was supposed to stand for.

Nevertheless, the 924 did have its strengths and, after that first uncharacteristic rush into production, it developed over its 13-year life-span into a first-rate sports coupé, able to display the famous Porsche crest with pride.

Very few companies are as constant and conscientious as Porsche in research and development. Very few cars are as painstakingly built. Quality materials and attention to detail are second to none, and the improvements brought with each new model year are rarely just cosmetic face-lifts but are developments which have been analysed and prepared in depth and make an appreciable difference. The evolution of the 924, through the 924 Turbo, the rare Carrera GT, and culminating in the 924S, is a story of unceasing endeavour.

By far the greatest single evolution out of the 924 range was the 944 model, effectively the 924's 'big brother'. Altogether racier in appearance, its bulging rear wheel arches and front wings matched to an all-new 163bhp 2.5-litre engine, the 944 started production in November 1981, with right-hand-drive models reaching the UK the following April. It was an instant success in Britain — helped, no doubt, by the country pulling out of the recession of the early 1980s and the Thatcher 'boom' getting under way.

Inside, early 944s were similar to the 924. There the resemblance ceased, however: to look at, and to drive, they offered Porsche buyers a whole new experience. Again, Porsche developed and redeveloped the 944 into one of the best all-round sports cars in the world. Its family line — the Lux, the Turbo, the 944S, the S2 and the Cabriolet — all demonstrated the company's willingness and ability to move with, and ahead of, the times.

Now the 944 itself is to be superceded by the much-revised new model — the 968 — whose success has yet to be proved but which has gained highly favourable early comment following its first appearance. The 968's seductive styling, its powerful equipment and improved handling, have all impressed.

Thanks to Porsche's success in widening its market, it can truthfully be said that owners come from all walks of life: they may have paid as little as £3,000 for an early 924 or as much as £70,000 for a new 911 Turbo. What they have in common is the appreciation of a great automobile — and a readiness to 'talk Porsche' whenever the opportunity arises.

The Reading headquarters of Porsche Cars Great Britain. The handsome interior courtyard makes a fine setting for the cars, especially, as pictured here, during the Christmas season.

Porsche Cars GB

Porsche GB's Reading premises are where the cars are prepared before being farmed out to the UK dealership. This includes de-waxing the cars in the steam-cleaning bay.

A few words about this book. Despite the formidable body of literature available on the marque, Porsche devotees will surely appreciate the fine examples portrayed in its pages; most are owned by Porsche Club Great Britain members and are in fully original condition.

For those who enthuse over the cars but have not yet got around to buying one, it is hoped that the book will describe and picture the cars in sufficient detail that their eventual choice of model will be better-informed and, ultimately, that much more rewarding. This is *not* just 'another picture book' (though you can take it that way if you like). Its aim is to inform, as well as to entertain.

Unlike some collectable cars one could name, the vast majority of 924s and 944s are used as everyday driving vehicles. Indeed, it is doubtful whether any other great sports car manufacturers have their cars driven quite so much by quite such a high percentage of owners. With long service intervals and with that aforementioned build quality and reliability, these are cars which *demand* to be driven. They are economical on fuel and there is a great trade in after-market services and spares, from both factory-approved and other outlets. Furthermore, there is a worldwide network of Porsche clubs, whose magazines feature numerous private and trade advertisements for both cars and parts. It is rarely that any Porsche need be off the road for long.

There has probably never been a better time to buy a 924 or 944 than now. As a glance at the classified section of any classic car magazine will confirm, there are plenty available and their prices reflect a sense of economic proportion which has not always been the case in the past. Hopefully, ownership of a Porsche can become a reality for many people who had previously regarded it as beyond their reach. Any of the four-cylinder, front-engined models has the potential to give enormous pleasure, and if this book can help enthusiasts choose the one most suited to their particular requirements, or play a small part in cementing their affinity to the marque, its job will have been done.

Replacing the 944, the 968 incorporates many new features and offers (at a price) superb looks and outstanding performance. It is available in both closed and open form.
Porsche Cars GB

Porsche Cars GB

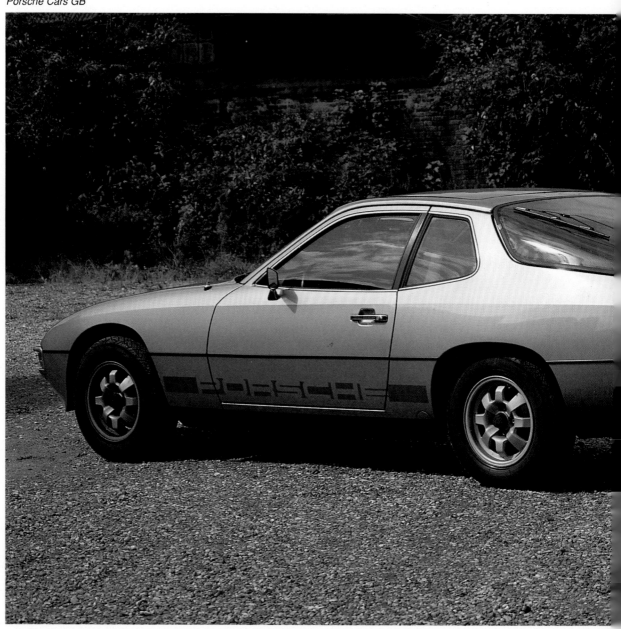

The Porsche 924

The very early 924s were relatively plain in appearance and in standard form were far from luxuriously equipped. They also suffered, as was pointed by road testers of the time, from limited accommodation, high noise level and (in the words of *Motor* magazine) 'poor bump-thump suppression'. Performance overall was praised, however, as was the highly economic fuel consumption... though eyebrows were raised at what was seen as a less-than-economic price-tag.

The 1977 model-year car had a galvanised steel chassis with six-year anti-corrosion guarantee. Only from 1980 was the entire bodyshell zinc-coated and the guarantee extended to seven years. This is worth bearing in mind when considering a pre-1980 car.

Service intervals were at 12,000 miles, with an oil-change at 6,000. When full, the 13.6-gallon petrol tank was good for at least 350 miles.

1977 models in basic form did not have tinted glass all round (only the rear window was tinted), a rear wiper, electric windows or mirrors, alloy wheels or a leatherbound steering-wheel. All these items were extra.

It was not until the 1978 model year (Porsche model years begin in the preceding August) that buyers were offered the option of a five-speed gearbox. A change for all 1978 cars was a revision to the rear suspension mounting which noticeably reduced vibration and noise.

Pictured here and on the previous page are two very well kept early 924s belonging to Porsche Club Great Britain members living in Bristol. Both are in one of Porsche's most popular colours, Guards Red.

OIB 2995, owned by Michael O'Regan, is a 1977 model with no extras apart from 'added afterwards' alloy wheels.

The lack of a five-speed gearbox is a distinct disadvantage on these 1977 cars. The same can be said of the lack of a rear window wiper — an optional extra which this car does not have — which leaves a huge area of glass unprotected against rain.

TAR 532R belongs to Brian Pitman and is a 1978 model. It has a host of extras, including a rear spoiler, electric windows, door mirrors and radio aerial and, unusually, air-conditioning and the three-speed automatic gearbox.

The 1977 car shows the chromed door-handles and side window strips, as well as the raised writing on the rear. Even 15 years on, the quality of the paintwork is evident. It still has an excellent finish and shine to it, and there is little sign of rust, despite the fact that 1977 models only had hot-dipped zinc-coated floor pans.

It did not take the UK importers long to realise that most, if not all, potential buyers wanted a higher level of specification as standard. Thus the 1978 model year saw the arrival of the 924 Lux. This included alloy 6J wheels with wider tyres, tinted windows all round, a rear window wiper and headlamp washers as standard, as well as electric windows, high-quality carpet and trim, front and rear anti-roll bars, built-in rear foglights and a leatherbound steering-wheel. The Lux cost £7,800, as against the base model's £7,350.

Other features for 1978 were the oval-shaped exhaust and the rubbing strip along the side of the car. The optional 'tilt' or 'lift-out' sunroof can also be seen. All in all, the 924 Lux was, and still is, an extremely attractive car.

Porsche Cars GB

1979 models saw the 924 Lux with electric windows and a heated and electrically operated driver's door mirror as standard. There were cloth inserts in the door panels for the first time.

It was not until the 1980 model year that the new five-speed gearbox with fifth gear to the right and forward of the 'H' was made standard. The previous five-speed gearbox, optional for 1978 and 1979, had first gear as a dog leg left of the 'H'.

The 924 continued to improve throughout its ten-year lifespan. Many of the changes were individually small, but their cumulative effect was one of increasing refinement. Improved soundproofing was a significant factor.

By the 1984 model year, there were redesigned door pockets and panels, small indicator lights between the front wheel arch and door, a flexible rear spoiler (1983) and syncromesh on reverse. 1984 saw the introduction of the electric rear tailgate release as standard and the electric tilt of the sunroof as an option. The Porsche motif was woven into the cloth inserts for the seats. These were the finishing touches to the 2-litre 924, prior to its replacement late in 1985 by the 2.5-litre 924S.

PORSCHE 924 1976-1985

Bodyshell:
Steel unitary construction 2-door hatchback coupé.
Zinc coating: floorpan initially, whole body from 1981.

Engine:
VW/Audi 4-cylinder in-line water-cooled. Iron block,
light-alloy cylinder head. Belt-driven single overhead
camshaft, 8 valves. Bore and stroke 86.5mm x
84.4mm, capacity 1,984cc, compression ratio 9.3:1.
Bosch K-Jetronic fuel injection. Power 125bhp at
5,800rpm, torque 121.5lb/ft at 3,500rpm.

Transmission:
Manual: engine-mounted clutch, rear-mounted gearbox
and differential. Audi 4-speed gearbox initially; Porsche
5-speed option from 1978; Audi 5-speed standard from
1980. Alternative VW 3-speed automatic option from
1977.

Suspension:
Front; VW 1303-derived MacPherson struts, coil
springs, Golf-derived lower wishbones. Rear; VW
1303-derived semi-trailing arms, transverse torsion
bars. Front and rear anti-roll bars optional initially,
standard from 1981. VW rack-and-pinion steering.

Brakes, wheels, tyres:
Solid discs front, drums rear, servo. 5 1/2J x 14 steel
wheels; 165 HR14 tyres. 6J x 14 light alloy wheels
optional, later standard; 185/70 HR14 tyres.

Dimensions:
Wheelbase 2,400mm/94.5in. Front track
1,418mm/55.8in. Rear track 1,372mm/54in. Length
4,213 to 4,320mm, 166 to 170in, according to bumper
type. Width 1,684mm/66.3in. Height 1,270mm/50in.

Performance:
0 to 100kph/62mph 10.5 seconds. Maximum
200kph/125mph.

Price at launch:
UK £6,999. USA $9,395.

Porsche Martini 924

As already noted, the 924 was produced by Porsche 'to appeal to a wider cross-section of potential Porsche owners', the price of the 911 having always been too high to attract more than a minority.

The £6,999 924 Coupé was therefore seen as the UK's first 'entry level' Porsche when it became available on March 10, 1977. On the same day, however, the factory released through Porsche Cars Great Britain (who had a few days earlier moved to superb new headquarters in Reading) the special specification '924 Celebration', or '924 Martini' as it has become better known.

The 'Martini' was nearly 10% dearer than the base model and had a very attractive 'standard' specification (see opposite page).

The example illustrated here is owned by Brian Moore, of Launceston, Cornwall, who obtained the then-battered car in a straight exhange for an equally poor Audi 100 Estate! It has been restored in painstaking detail, keeping it totally original.

The immaculate condition of this car, its high level of specification, interior and exterior colour schemes, and of course its rarity value, make it an appreciating asset as well as an irresistible object in its own right.

Similar to the 1977 924 in all mechanical details, the 'Martini' came with a fully equipped interior package and special paintwork in the racing colours of the Martini-Porsche factory entries — white, with blue and red side-winders.

185/70 HR14 tyres were fitted to specially painted 6Jx14 white alloy wheels. Sports, leather-covered steering-wheel and front and rear anti-roll bars were further distinguishing features, as were tinted glass, headlamp washers and rear window-wiper.

The front and rear seats had a red central inlay with blue stitched piping and Martini-colours strip on the front-seat headrests.

The interior carpeting, including the luggage space, was also in red and a special commemorative World Championship plaque was located on the centre console.

Production was limited to just 1,000 worldwide, of which 100 were right-hand drive. The 'Martini' went on sale in the UK in March 1977, priced at £7,672.86

Note: potential buyers should not be taken in by an early 924 with added-later Martini stripes. Always check interior, specification and chassis number to ensure that you are being shown the genuine article.

Porsche 924 Turbo

Porsche Cars GB

First details of the turbo-charged 924 were released in November 1978, but it was not until exactly a year later that the first right-hand-drive examples were introduced in the UK. The Turbo was considerably more expensive: £13,629, as against £9,582 for the 924 Lux. It was, though, a very different car.

Porsche had not been content simply to add a turbo and some 'go faster' stripes. The engineers had looked at the car from every angle and upgraded everything they felt necessary. The brake horsepower of the Turbo was 170, against the standard car's 125bhp — a 36 percent increase, and it certainly showed on the open road.

The 924 Turbo is easily identified by the four cooling vents between the headlight covers and the very neat and beautifully shaped duct in the bonnet. There were more air-ducts built into the front spoiler to further help cooling of the engine.

There was a rubber rear spoiler and unusual multi-spoke alloy wheels which — concours entrants please note — are a brute to clean.

Also featured were a separate oil cooler, two fuel pumps, bigger driveshafts, strengthened half-shafts and rear ventilated disc brakes. Stronger hubs provided a five-bolt wheel mounting instead of the less powerful car's four-bolt arrangement. The springs, anti-roll bars and shock absorbers were upgraded. The standard five-speed gearbox retained the dog-leg first gear of the ordinary 924. Standard items included a quality Panasonic stero with electric aerial, tinted glass all round, headlamp washers and a rear wiper.

Aesthetically pleasing, very fast, economical and with excellent handling and roadholding, as well as a high level of standard equipment, the Turbo is a thoroughly impressive driving machine. When new, it was almost as expensive as a 911SC, but it now represents exceptional value secondhand.

Previous page and above: This 1980 model-year 924 Turbo belongs to Terry Pitt, of Wellington, Somerset. The pictures clearly reveal the car's neat lines, set off by the spoked alloy wheels and Porsche side-lettering. The chequered upholstery can just be seen in the rear-view shot.

Though first registered on August 1 1980, it appears to be a 1980 model-year car as it does not have the side indicator flashers, between the front wheel arch and door, which the 1981 cars have. The 1981 car's engine output was up 7bhp to 177. The turbo unit was smaller and likely to last significantly longer due to better crankcase breathing improving oil circulation after switching off the ignition. Other improvements were minor, such as Porsche lettering on the door panels, a brake fluid level indicator and a larger fuel tank.

1982 was the last year of manufacture of the 924 Turbo, the introduction of the 944 in Europe at the end of 1981 effectively killing it off.

Very few changes were introduced for the 1982 car. A significant option, however, were the smart (and very easily cleaned) 928-style alloy wheels. New upholstery, carpeted door pockets and a Porsche crest on the glove compartment catch were the only 'improvements'.

Porsche Cars GB

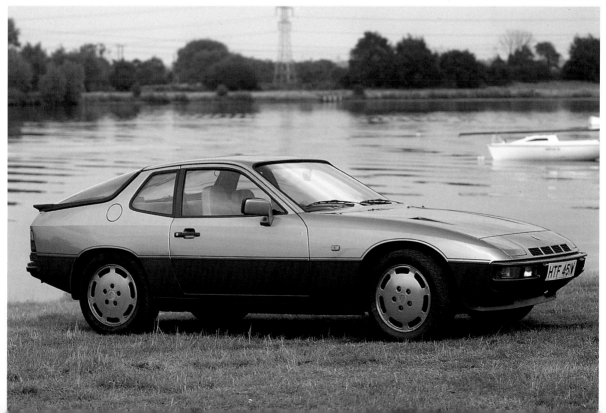

PORSCHE 924 TURBO 1978-1982

As 924 except:

Engine:

Detail revisions include new cylinder head. KKK turbocharger. Initial specification: compression ratio 7.5:1, power 170bhp at 5,500rpm, torque 181lb/ft at 3,500rpm. From mid-1980: smaller turbo, digital ignition, compression ratio 8.5:1, power 177bhp at 5,500rpm, torque 184lb/ft at 3,500rpm.

Transmission:

Porsche 5-speed gearbox, no alternatives.

Suspension:

Uprated and strengthened. Anti-roll bars standard. 5-bolt hubs.

Brakes, wheels, tyres:

Ventilated discs front and rear, servo. 6J x 15 light alloy wheels, 185/70 VR15 tyres.

Performance:

0 to 100kph/62mph 7.8 seconds. Maximum 225kph/140mph.

Price at launch:

UK £13,629. USA $20,875.

Burt Gear, of Ilfracombe, owns this 1982 924 Turbo which is an excellent example of the breed. It is in an unusual two-tone beige (unusual probably because it is not as distinctive as the other two-tone colours available as an option). Note the air-ducts and side indicator flasher.

739 LMG

Porsche 924 Carrera GT

This is very nearly the rarest water-cooled Porsche, be it 924, 944 or 928.

First shown at the 1979 Frankfurt Motor Show as a highly developed 924 Turbo, the Carrera GT evolved into a homologation special with a limited production run of 406, including six prototypes. Of these, 190 remained in Germany, 75 right-hand-drive examples came to the UK, and the remaining 135 were spread across the rest of Europe. None went to America.

The nose air ducts are the same as on the 924 Turbo, but there is a much more purposeful air intake on the bonnet. The rear spoiler is larger, differently shaped and less flexible than the Turbo's. The front spoiler, however, is of lightweight flexible material and incorporates a single horizontal slot as opposed to the Turbo's rigid front spoiler with short, vertical air vents.

Other external differences can be seen in the front wing and rear wheel arch extension, which are of glass-filled flexible polyurethane, the polished and colour coded wheels, rear wheel arch spat and large, low profile tyres. The UK specification included electric windows, Panasonic radio/cassette player, tinted glass, rear wiper and electric driver's door mirror. Options included air conditioning or a steel sunroof, and a limited-slip differential.

Developed from the 'customer' GT, two more specialised versions appeared, the 245bhp GTS (40 built) and the amazing 375bhp GTR (19 built). Both were available only in left-hand drive and for 'special' customers.

These models are distinguishable from the standard GT by the transparent covers over their non-pop-up headlights. Customer GTS models were available only in red and GTRs only in white.

PORSCHE 924 CARRERA GT 1980

Limited-production evolution from 924 Turbo.

Bodyshell:
Polyurethane front wings and rear wheelarch flares.

Engine:
Modifications include strengthened crankshaft and revised cylinder head. Intercooler. Digital ignition. Compression ratio 8.5:1, power 210bhp at 6,000rpm, torque 203lb/ft at 3,500rpm.

Wheels and tyres:
Forged aluminium wheels. Standard; 7J x 15 rims, 215/60 VR 15 tyres. Optional: front 7J x 16 rims, 205/55 VR 16 tyres; rear 8J x 16 rims, 225/50 VR16 tyres.

Dimensions:
Front track 1,477mm/58.2in. Rear track 1,476mm/58.1in. Width 1,737mm/68.4in.

Performance:
0 to 100kph/62mph 6.9 seconds. Maximum 240kph/150mph.

Price at launch:
UK £19,211.

The original Carrera GT sold out within just a few weeks, its desirability boosted, no doubt, by the fact that three factory-prepared versions had achieved sixth, twelfth and thirteenth on their first and only appearance in the Le Mans 24-Hour Race, in 1980.

The 924 Carrera GT has a superb racing pedigree. Its lightweight materials and 210 bhp turbocharged engine with air-to-air intercooler make it one of *the* Porsches to own — the equivalent, if you like, of the RS Carrera version of the 911.

Race driver and five-times Le Mans winner Derek Bell received a
924 Carrera GTS in 1982 as part of his contract with Porsche.
Disappointed at first — he had wanted neither a 924 nor a red
Porsche — he later described it to *911 & Porsche World* as the
best-handling road car he had ever driven. 'The best thing about it
is at 100mph it's not on boost. It sits there at 4000 revs, off boost,
28 miles to the gallon and you're cruising at 100mph!'

Mike Valente

Walter Rohrl and Christian Geistdorfer, world rally champions (for Fiat) in 1980, occasionally drove this works-prepared Carrera 924 GTR as private entrants in European rallies.

Porsche Cars GB

Porsche 924S

With the S model given the detuned (from 163 to 150bhp) 944 2.5-litre engine, the 924 was finally provided with the power unit it had been crying out for. The added power and torque of the 944 engine, one of the smoothest four-cylinders available anywhere, resulted in a truly excellent Grand Touring coupé. It was economical, powerful and quiet. In fact, you would hardly recognise from inside the difference between the 924S and the early 944.

Pictured on these pages is an immaculate 1986 example owned by PCGB member Cliff Randell.

The 924 shape, as it evolved with the smart rear spoiler, alloy wheels and other Porsche niceties, makes it in many people's eyes more attractive than the more 'macho' 944 — though this is obviously a matter of personal taste rather than of any objective criteria.

The car's only minus is that it retained the antiquated 924/early 944-style dashboard (see 'Interiors', further on this book). But perhaps that is not surprising, bearing in mind that Porsche were to axe the car by August 1988.

This 1987 924S belongs to another PCGB member, Colin Bryant, of Alveston, Avon. It boasts the standard early 928-style 'telephone dial' alloy wheels and the smart but discreet 'S' logo along the side sill. This car also has the optional power-assisted steering — a great asset, particularly as the 924's wheels and tyres grew larger over the years, making parking and other manoeuvres considerably more onerous.

Significant improvements were made to the 924S in its last year of production, with the introduction of the 160bhp 944 engine, power steering as standard and a split rear-seat backrest. It is a shame these useful changes occurred in the twilight of its existence. If you can find one, the 1988 model is a highly rewarding car.

The tilt or lift-out sunroof was an expensive option when buying a 924 (or 944) new. It did not in fact slide: the back just tilted a few inches, and the only alternative was to stop and lift out the entire panel — not always a simple task, especially on a main road or motorway. When buying used, however, the sunroof is a desirable feature, and it should be noted that from 1984 an electric tilt facility was available.

PORSCHE 924S 1985-1988

Essentially 924 'narrow' body with 944 engine and running gear.

Bodyshell:

As 924, with revised polyurethane front skirt and rear under-body spoiler/diffuser.

Engine:

2,479cc Porsche 4-cylinder as 944. Initial specification: compression ratio 9.7:1, power 150bhp at 5,800rpm, torque 144lb/ft at 3,000rpm. For 1988: compression ratio 10.5:1, power 160bhp at 5,900rpm, torque 155lb/ft at 4,500rpm.

Transmission:

As 944, manual or optional automatic.

Suspension:

As 944, with cast light alloy wishbones and trailing arms.

Brakes, wheels, tyres:

As 944. Standard; 6J x 15 light alloy wheels, 195/65 VR15 tyres. Optional; 6J x 16 forged aluminium wheels, 195/55 VR16 tyres.

Dimensions: As 924.

Performance:

0 to 100kph/62mph 8.2 seconds. Maximum 219kph/137mph.

Price at launch:

UK £14,985. USA $19,900.

Porsche 924S 'Le Mans'

It is slightly ironic that Porsche should introduce significant limited edition 924s into the UK in only the first and final years of production. First, as already seen, was the Celebration or Martini 924; second came the 1988 924S 'Le Mans'. Only 74 were sold in the UK, half in Alpine white, half in black.

(Perhaps one should mention here two other limited edition models, though they differed from the standard car in only a few cosmetic details. The 'Dubloon' (1979), of which only 50 were built, featured gold metallic paintwork with pinstripe interior. In 1980, Porsche celebrated the 924's successful debut at Le Mans by adding a few features to the 924 Lux — 924 Turbo wheels, 60-series low profile tyres, Alpine white paintwork with gold, red and black coachline, and a discreet Le Mans logo on the front wings. It was called, predictably enough, the 924 Le Mans.)

The 'Le Mans' car inherited from the 924S both its 160bhp 944 engine and power steering as standard. The rear seat backrest was split and a special luggage cover which lifted with the tailgate was optional.

The model also came with sport suspension, including gas filled shock absorbers, lower ride height, harder springs and a larger rear anti-roll bar. 7J wheels, with colour coded high-lights matching the interior colour, were fitted. The 'Le Mans' side-writing looked smart in contrasting colour to the body.

Inside, the 37 black cars had grey flannel cloth with a turquoise stripe; the 37 white cars, grey with an ochre stripe.

Its rarity, its quality design and engineering and its performance on the road, all combine to make the car a serious collector's item.

Production of 924s closed in August 1988, 13 years after it had begun and just over 11 years after the introduction of the first right-hand-drive cars.

Porsche 944

Porsche Cars GB

When the 944 was launched in November 1981, the 924 had been in production almost six years. Almost six months later, in April 1982, the 944 appeared for the first time in right-hand-drive form.

From its rather basic beginnings, the 924 had been refined into an attractive and well-equipped sports model, the Turbo version being a true performance car and the Carrera GT selling out within a few weeks of being announced. Porsche were confident, therefore, that there would be a strong market for a more aggressive, 'macho' model, particularly among successful, or up and coming, business people. The more expensive 911 was not seen by many as a vehicle which they would want as their only car, while the 924 was continuing to attract buyers who wanted their one, or main, car to be a step up from the GTi-style hot hatchbacks of the era.

The 944 was seen as a car which existed conveniently between these two extremes: less costly than the 911, it would be a highly acceptable 'everyday' car, yet it was also a visible notch higher than the 924. It was felt that not only owners of rival cars, but also current 924 owners, would be interested. And, perhaps, possessors of a 911 or 928 would be attracted to it as a desirable second car for use as daily transport.

Nearly 14,000 944s were produced in 1982, climbing to over 24,500 in 1983, 1984 and 1985. Porsche mania was well underway, especially in the UK, where jokes involving yuppies and Porsches abounded by the mid-1980s.

The immaculate 1983 model shown here belongs to PCGB member, David Pipes. Note the protective side strip which was the only external change from the previous year. It shares with the 1982 car the smooth, all aluminium water-cooled four-cylinder in-line engine. The bodywork carries a seven-year Longlife guarantee. The polyurethrane front spoiler, combined with the bulging front and rear wheel arches (smoothed off and integral within the body shape, compared to the 'added on' look of the 924 Carrera GT) give the car a strongly purposeful appearance, in keeping with Porsche's image.

The pop-up headlights were unusual at the time, but were copied by most of the Japanese coupés; hence their abandonment in the Porsche's brand-new successor, the 968.

Multi-cluster rear tail-lights were a lifelong feature of both the 924 and 944. The 'Rubik cube' layout is both smart and effective.

PORSCHE 944 1982-1989

Bodyshell:
Zinc-protected steel unitary 2-door hatchback coupe, evolved from 924 with widened wings front and rear.

Engine:
Porsche-designed 4-cylinder in-line water-cooled (effectively half 928 V8 engine). Light alloy construction. Belt-driven single overhead camshaft, 8 valves. Twin contra-rotating balancer shafts. Bosch Motronic engine management. Bore and stroke 100mm x 78.9mm, capacity 2,479cc; 1989 104mm x 78.9mm, 2,681cc. Compression ratio 10.6:1; 1988 10.2:1; 1989 10.9:1. Power 163bhp at 5,800rpm; 1988 160bhp at 5,900rpm; 1989 165bhp at 5,800rpm. Torque 151lb/ft at 3,500rpm; 1988 155lb/ft at 4,500rpm; 1989 166lb/ft at 4,200rpm.

Transmission:
Rear-mounted Audi 5-speed manual gearbox or optional VW 3-speed automatic.

Suspension:
Front; MacPherson struts, coil springs, lower wishbones, anti-roll bar. Rear; semi-trailing arms, transverse torsion bars, anti-roll bar. Cast light alloy wishbones and trailing arms replace fabricated steel from 1986. ZF rack-and-pinion steering, power assistance optional for 1984, standard from 1985.

Brakes, wheels, tyres:
Ventilated discs front and rear, servo; ABS optional from 1987. 7J x 15 light alloy wheels, 185/70 VR15 tyres standard, 215/60 VR15 optional. Other options; 7J x 16, later 7J front and 8J rear, 205/55 and 225/50 VR16 tyres

Dimensions:
Wheelbase 2,400mm/94.5in. Front track 1,478mm/58.2in. Rear track 1,450mm/57.1in. Length 4,200 to 4,320mm, 165.3 to 170in, according to bumper type. Width 1,735mm/68.3in. Height 1,275mm/50.2in.

Performance:
0 to 100kph/62mph 8.4 seconds. Maximum 220kph/137mph.

Price at launch:
UK £12,999. USA $18,450.

Porsche Cars GB

On the 1984 car, it was possible to release the rear tailgate electrically from inside. This may sound a minor improvement, but with the lock nestling under the protruding rear spoiler, unlocking manually had been a frustratingly fiddly operation, especially at night and in unfriendly weather.

The large and expensive sunroof gained an electric tilt in 1984. Colour-coded wheel centres in black, white or platinum became an option on the forged alloy wheels. Cruise control was also an option, though probably less than appealing to the average Porsche owner, as it destroys the feedback element which drivers of high-performance cars regard as an indispensable pleasure.

Registered in August 1986, PCGB member Dave Bignell's metallic grey 944 Lux, with burgundy pinstripe interior, has the early 928-style 'telephone dial' alloy wheels, with 215/60 VR15 optional-extra tyres. It also boasts the new oval dashboard, a real leap ahead in updating the 944's interior. By now, virtually everything was operated electrically — windows, mirrors, seats, sunroof tilt, rear hatch — while power steering had been standard since the previous year. A top-tinted windscreen, removable radio/cassette and integral front and rear foglights make up the high specification of this example.

Through 1987 and 1988, the 944 underwent few changes. The number of options grew dramatically, however. As new, a 'fully-loaded' (i.e. very high specification) Porsche would have cost its owner a considerable sum above and beyond the car's base price, and this difference will not be fully reflected in its secondhand value. Such a car will, though, be easier to re-sell later — and will have provided its second owner with the enjoyment of a more personalized 944 (or 924) in the meantime. (Sight of the original invoice is the only sure means of ascertaining which features were standard and which optional.)

A Limited Edition model, of which 30 came into the UK, in Zermatt silver celebrated the 100,000th 944 built. Most 'extras' were standard; in addition, a special grey interior, an automatic heating control, wider wheels and a split rear seat were fitted.

Guy Hall is the owner of this perfect 1988 2.5-litre 944 Lux. Outwardly, it displays little change from either the 1986 or 1987 models. There has been further 'tweeking' of standard extras and a slight decrease in bhp to 160. Catalytic converters were fitted for many countries, though not the UK.

Porsche 944 Turbo

Often dimissed by those who have never had the chance to drive it, the 944 Turbo launched in the summer of 1985 is right up there in the junior supercar league. In the words of *Motor* magazine: 'It's as fast as a 911 Carrera, as roomy as a 928S, and more fuel-efficient than either. Even by supercar standards, packages don't come much more formidable than that.'

Nor was such enthusiasm confined to just one side of the Atlantic. The influential US monthly, *Road & Track*, stated that 'The Turbo was magnificent... not only the best 944 ever, but one of the best Porsches' and lamented the fact that America would be taking in only half of the first year's 7,200 production total.

PCGB member Ken Booty lived in Germany for some time and bought his high-specification early 944 Turbo there, importing it into the UK in March 1991. The rear under-spoiler helped keep the rear tyres well and truly gripping the road, even at speeds in excess of 150mph. In April 1986 the author saw 175mph on the speedometer on an empty autobahn while visiting the Nürburgring and the Porsche factory in Stuttgart, and managed to squeeze 290 miles into just two hours' travelling. The only intrusive noise was a very slight whistle at the rear of the closed sunroof. Fuel consumption was economical, averaging nearly 30mpg over 2500 miles.

At time of writing, an immaculate early Turbo can be purchased for less than £15,000 and is a sound buy.

PORSCHE 944 TURBO 1985-1991

As 944 except:

Bodyshell:

Revised nose moulding and under-body spoiler/diffuser at rear.

Engine:

KKK water-cooled turbocharger. Compression ratio 8:1. Power 220bhp at 5,800rpm; from 1989 250bhp at 6,500rpm. Torque 243lb/ft at 3,500rpm; from 1989 258lb/ft at 4,000rpm.

Transmission:

Strengthened gearbox, no automatic option.

Wheels and tyres:

Cast light alloy 16in wheels, 7J front and 8J rear, 205/55 and 225/50 VR16 tyres. Forged light alloy wheels optional.

Performance:

0 to 100kph/62mph 6.3 seconds. Maximum 245kph/152mph.

Price at launch:

UK £25,311. USA $30,000.

Photos Porsche Cars GB

The 1987 model had anti-lock brakes (ABS) and electric adjustment of driver and passenger seats as standard. Other refinements included automatic climate control and an integral windscreen aerial for the four-speaker radio/ cassette system. The following year, the spoked forged wheels were standard equipment.

Photos Porsche Cars GB

A Sport Equipment model, limited to just 1,000, appeared in November 1987. Only 70 came into the UK in right-hand-drive form. They were in Silver Fox metallic, with the 250bhp engine, a special interior and heated front seats and a split rear seat backrest as standard. Cost was more than £41,000.

The 1990 944 Turbo featured the smoother, disc-style wheels and a wing rear spoiler — a great improvement on the previous type, which had first been seen on 924s in the mid-1970s.

Below: Note the towbar on PCGB member Ian Iles' car. An expensive addition — on the motorway with powerboat hitched up, it must be an impressive spectacle.

Porsche Cars GB

911 & Porsche World

The 944 Turbo Cabriolet was launched in February 1991 with production of right-hand-drive models limited to just 100. The 250bhp 2.5-litre engine is the same as in the 944 Turbo Coupé which campaigned in the 944 Turbo Cup racing series in Europe, South Africa and Canada, giving a top speed of over 160mph and a 0-62.5mph time of less than six seconds. It is also claimed that the car can be stopped from 62.5mph in only three seconds.

Porsche 944S

Following the amazingly consistent sales achieved during the three previous years, the 944 Lux dipped by more than half in 1986, with sales totalling just 11,800 units. Considerable hope, therefore, was placed on the 944S. Launched in the late summer of 1986, its four valves per cylinder 190bhp engine provided a small improvement in performance, but no more than that. At £24,000, it was almost double the price of the original 944, introduced just four years earlier.

Photos Porsche Cars GB

PORSCHE 944S 1987-1989

As 944 except:

Engine:

Twin overhead camshafts, 16 valves. Compression ratio 10.9:1, power 190bhp at 6,000rpm, torque 170lb/ft at 4,300rpm.

Transmission:

As 944 Turbo.

Performance:

0 to 100kph/62mph 7.9 seconds. Maximum 228kph/142mph.

Price at launch:

UK £23,977.

By the time the Series 2 944 was launched in early 1989, Porsche prices had climbed even further and the new model cost a hefty £31,000-plus. But this time the improvement in performance was more significant. The engine had been extensively redesigned, increased in capacity to three litres, and now pushed out 211bhp, ample for a series-production road car — though still only 1bhp more than the 924 Carrera GT back in 1981.

As can be seen in the ultra-smooth and rounded lines of PCGB members Martin Simon's February 1990 Series 2 Cabriolet and Peter Sealey's August 1990 model (with matching peacock!), the Series 2 also had a 'new look'.

Particularly attractive are the rounded boot and front end treatment of the Series 2; but further price rises at the end of the 1980s had a knock-on effect on Porsche sales, both new and secondhand.

The Cabriolet version came with a boot and no spoiler, of course, which resulted in far cleaner lines. (The full circle from boot to hatchback and back to boot again has been a recurring theme in car design in recent decades, and in purely aesthetic terms it is almost invariably the booted version which comes out best.) Of all the later model 944s, the Cabriolet currently represents one of the better buys second-hand (admittedly at the higher end of the scale, but compare its price used with the staggering £39,000 new price in 1990).

PORSCHE 944S2 1989-1991
As 944 except:
Bodyshell:
Turbo-style nose and tail. Alternative Cabriolet has reinforced floorpan, lower windscreen, bootlid in place of rear hatch.
Engine:
Twin overhead camshafts, 16 valves. Bore and stroke 104mm x 88mm, capacity 2,990cc, compression ratio 10.9:1. Power 211bhp at 5,800rpm, torque 207lb/ft at 4,000rpm.
Transmission:
As 944 Turbo.
Wheels and tyres:
Forged light alloy 16in wheels, 7J front and 8J rear, 205/55 and 225/50 VR16 tyres.
Performance:
0 to 100kph/62mph 6.9 seconds. Maximum 240kph/149mph.
Price at launch:
UK £31,304. USA $45,998.

Its buyers at least obtained electric operation of the hood for their money, though still being required manually to clamp the hood fast against the top rail of the windscreen once the hood had descended.

With its hood in place, the Cabriolet is a truly beautiful looking car. In the American Porsche magazine, *Excellence*, Dave Colman commented:

'For those Porsche enthusiasts looking for an investment quality 944 with a flair for elegance, the S2 Cabriolet is the instrument of choice.'

Evolution:
Porsche 924 & 944

Research and development are *the* major components of Porsche philosophy. Regardless of the degree of success achieved, the appearance of a new model is no more than a stepping-stone towards further refinements aimed at increasing both performance and reliability.

It should not be forgotten that the first 924 was a 'rush job', originally designed by Porsche to be the new Volkswagen sports coupé. There were only a few brief months between Porsche's effectively taking over the design in the spring of 1975 and the appearance of the first cars off the production line. Consequently, the early 924s were not as near 'launch perfection' as Porsche would have wished.

The illustration left shows the rounded, spoilerless shape of the early 924 in the far background; then the later model with rear spoiler. The bulging rear wheel arch and larger rear spoiler is evident in the 944 and is clearly illustrated in the black 944 Turbo in the foreground.

Above: how the 924 Carrera GT in the middle evolved out of the rounded 924 and subsequently into the aggressive 944. The Carrera sits between a 1986 924S and a 1990 944 Turbo. The 924 front end is slender and smoothly pointed, while that of the 944, particularly of later years, is fuller and more rounded.

Above: a 1987 model year 944 Lux alongside a 1986 model year 944 Turbo. The latter has a more rounded and less fussy front bumper and light cluster, illustrative of the way Porsche introduces small but significant changes which then filter through the range later on. (Although a year earlier than the Lux, the Turbo has the more modern front of the two.) Rear view of the same cars (left): the under-bumper rear spoiler and slightly different top spoiler are shown.

This page: 924 Carrera GT and 944. Rear, front and side views clearly illustrate the changes — and the affinities — in cars which are 10 years apart.

Wheels

Right: One of the first colour coded wheels was featured on the limited-edition 924 Martini/Celebration model of 1977. Note considerable clearance between tyre and wheel arch and the very understated Porsche insignia on the rubberised centre cap.

Left: The standard 924 wheel was of steel, with this 6Jx14 alloy wheel still available only as an option in 1978. It has a smart Porsche crest in the centre and four-bolt fixing.

Left: The fabulous 911-style Fuchs forged five-spoke 7Jx15 wheel of the 924 Carerra GT. This one has had the rim polished and the centre colour coded with the alloy centre crest highlighted in Porsche colours.

Right: The standard 6Jx15 cast alloy wheel fitted to the 924 Turbo throughout its three-year life in the UK. The five fixing bolts are sunk well into the wheel and the spokes are fine and multiple — a nightmare to clean, but difficult to avoid if you wish to keep your 924 Turbo original. The only exception is the 1982 model, which provided the option of 928-style 16-inch wheels.

Right: The 924S had wheels in the style of the original 928. Smart and easier to clean, these are commonly referred to as 'telephone dial' wheels. The Porsche crest is unpainted and somewhat drab. Owners of earlier cars frequently painted the wheel centres to show off the crest in its attractive factory colours, but on the 924S and 924 Turbo this is not really an option: the crest is cast with a rough, crinkly finish and large parts of it are in black.

Right: 1983 944 Lux had the 'cookie-cutter' wheel, so named because of its similarity to the kitchen utensil. It is one of the least attractive within the range.

Left: 944 Lux launched in August 1988 shows how Porsche persisted with the 1978 928-style alloy wheel design for 10 years. On younger cars, it looks rather dated.

In fact, the factory provided some very modern, clean-line alloy wheels — initially as an option — for the 1987 944 Turbo. By 1988 they were standard on the Turbo and a year later on the S2. The wheel pictured right is on a 1990 944 Turbo and has an unpainted centre crest, while that shown below is on a 1991 944 Cabriolet special edition model with the smarter, factory-painted centre.

Aftermarket accessories are big business, though perhaps less so with Porsche than with some other manufacturers. The BBS wheel illustrated here is fitted to a left-hand-drive German specification 1985 944 Turbo and, with the car being in black, matches it well. Clearly, however, a concours judge would not like it, and should the car come up for sale, some would see it as a definite minus. As a general rule, it is wise not to over-personalise your Porsche.

Spoilers

Opposite and above: Porsche
began with no spoiler on the
rear of the 924 and finished
with two rear spoilers on the
944 Turbo. The spoilers grew
larger throughout the two
models' development. A rear
under-bumper spoiler was first
seen with the introduction of
the 944 Turbo in the summer of
1985. It not only ensured anti-
lift of the rear end but assisted
with the cooling of the transmission, exhaust and fuel tank.

Right, above and below:
Illustrated in close-up are rear
spoilers on the 924 Carrera GT
and 1982 924 Turbo.

Interiors

This page: The interior of the 924 showed little change during its 13-year history. What may have appeared modern in 1977 (right) looked decidedly old-hat in the 1987 924S (below). Almost certainly, the dated dashboard in particular lost the 924 a good many sales, especially after the introduction in 1985 of the more contemporary oval-shaped dashboard for the 944 Turbo.

Porsche Cars GB

Left: The 911-style high-back seats in this 1986 924S are extremely comfortable.

Below: 1982 924 Turbo fitted with 911 sports seats (not a factory option). Note the much more pronounced side-bolsters which grip the occupant. (Note also below and opposite the smaller, leather-covered steering wheel, as compared to the three-spoke wheel, opposite above.)

This page: A sombre interior lends itself to customising, as proved by these pictures of the author's 924 Carrera GT. The original Carrera GT displayed by Porsche at the 1979 Frankfurt Motor Show was also in red. The previous owner of the author's car followed suit, finding that the production model's interior — black with red pinstripe, 911 sports seats and all black carpeting and side panels — had a decidedly claustrophobic effect. Here, the light grey inserts combined with the red show off the all-leather interior, while the carpeting and side panels, together with the leather gear-lever gait and steering wheel, make the interior substantially lighter and more open. The gold plaque on the glove compartment is in recognition of the author's chairmanship of the Porsche Club Great Britain Concours in 1989.

Right: Early 944s had the same dashboard as the 924. As shown in this 1983 944 Lux, the smaller diameter steering wheel obscures most of the warning binnacle on the left and most (though not the important red line) of the rev counter on the right. Reflection is not too much of a problem. Heater controls are easy to read and operate on the centre console. Oil pressure, clock and ammeter are out of direct vision. Pedals are conventional pendant type, not sprouting from the floor as on the 911.

Right: 1985 944 Turbo — a German specification car with all-burgundy interior. The improvement wrought by the new dashboard shape is clear to see.

Right: Standard interior of this 1987 944 Lux shows the smart burgundy pinstripe carried through to the door panels. The quality of the finish and fine condition of the interior after four years' use are notable.

For owners wishing to keep their cars in the best possible condition, high-quality original materials are vital. Pictured here are a 1990 944 Turbo (above) and 1990 944 S2 Cabriolet (left). Note in both illustrations the aerated leather upholstery and in the lower picture the two hood handles stored in the door pocket.

Bottom left: Compare this with the picture at top of previous page to see how the 944 dashboard evolved. The white-on-black instruments with red needles are easy to read and only the water temperature gauge is obscured by the steering wheel. The air vents are massive by comparison with the earlier cars. The entire concept is cleaner and more contemporary.

Little things mean a lot — as evidenced by these interior door handles. Those in the 1985 944 Turbo and 1989 Lux (below right and bottom) are of incomparably neater design than in the 1981 924 Carrera GT (top).

Note the Porsche lettering on the door panel and 'Turbo' steel sill plate in the Carrera picture. The door pocket/armrest had grown an additional pocket by the time the 1985 model appeared; also visible are the electrically operated sports seats with their accentuated side bolster.

Left, above and below: Rear seating (1978 924 and 1987 924S). Whilst all 924s and 944s are 2+2s, only a very small or foolhardy adult would undertake to travel far as a rear-seat passenger. Even so, accommodation is distinctly better than in the 911 and at least provides for emergencies. For children aged up to nine or ten, it is quite adequate.

Left: the 'security cover' is rolled across the large luggage area of the 1982 924 Turbo…

...The full extent of the area is revealed in the 924 Carrera GT (top right). Also shown are the tool roll and the air compressor which plugs into the cigarette lighter and blows up the 'space saver' spare tyre housed beneath the luggage compartment floor. The handbook, which also includes the important 'service history' record, is shown above the plastic wallet containing the list of Porsche dealers worldwide and the radio stereo operation manual. Either side of the area are bins for storing valuables etc. out of sight under the carpeting.

(Note: On the subject of 'service history', never buy a used Porsche without a full, and substantiated, record.)

Right: Boot on the 944 S2 Cabriolet provides less accommodation than its hatchback stablemates. It is still sufficient, however, for a (reasonably) Grand Tour.

Right: Rear seat backrest folds down to provide further luggage space. The built-in security cover which rolls into the backrest forms a useful 'lip' to prevent luggage from sliding forward.

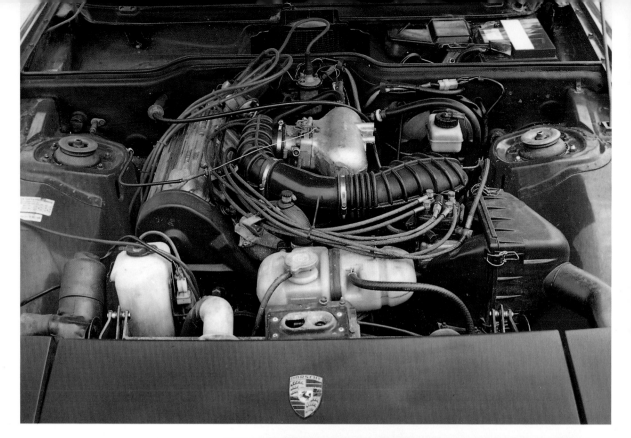

Engines

Above: 1977 Porsche 924. 1984cc producing 125bhp at 5800rpm, a top speed of 125mph and 0-62.5mph in 10.5 seconds.

Right: 1977 Porsche 924 Martini/Celebration. No change from the standard engine, but still in excellent condition after 15 years, as is the rest of the car (see photographs in chapter one).

Bottom right: 1981 Porsche 924 Carrera GT. With 210bhp at 6000rpm producing a top speed of 150mph and 0-62.5mph in 6.9 seconds, the Carrera was on a par with 911 performance standards. Fuel consumption was also good. The air-to-air intercooler can easily be seen, fitted over the camshaft cover.

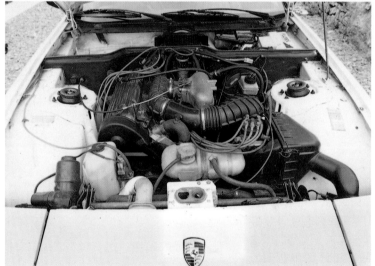

Left: 1982 Porsche 924 Turbo. Again the 1984cc engine, but now developing 177bhp at 5500rpm. (1979 and 1980 Turbos developed 170bhp at 5500rpm.) Top speed is 140mph, with a 0-62.5mph time of 7.8 seconds. The turbo unit was smaller on 1981/82 models, which both improved fuel consumption and enhanced the life of the turbo unit itself through better crankcase breathing.

Below: 1985 Porsche 944 Turbo. Shown in superb condition, this 2479cc engine developed 220bhp at 5800rpm, achieving a top speed of 152mph and accelerating from 0 to 62.5mph in just 6.3 seconds. The car's speed, handling and low noise-level are due in no small part to the smooth delivery of power right through the rev range.

Left and below: 1986 and 1988 Porsche 944 Lux. Developing 163bhp from 5800rpm, with a top speed of 137mph and 0-62.5mph acceleration in 8.4 seconds, this 2479cc engine was introduced in 1981 and used through to the summer of 1988, when it was briefly replaced by a 2.7-litre engine. It has two balance shafts which run at twice the engine's speed and counter-rotate; this Japanese-patented system gave the four-cylinder 944 six-cylinder smoothness. There is a Bosch L-Jetronic fuel system and the Bosch Motronic engine management system. The 2.7-litre engine brought an improvement in mid-range torque but achieved little overall change in performance. It was discontinued in the summer of 1989, by which time the Series 2 944 was well underway.

Below: 1990 Porsche 944 Series 2 Cabriolet. The engine is now three litres (2990cc), developing 211bhp at 5800rpm (with or without a catalytic converter) and running on unleaded fuel. Top speed is 149mph with 0-62.5mph achieved in 7.1 seconds.

The only other significant change during the life of the 944 was the introduction in August 1986 of a four valves per cylinder, twin overhead camshaft 2.5-litre engine developing 190bhp (midway between the 944's 163bhp and the Turbo's 220bhp) at 6000rpm. This boosted top speed from 137 to 142mph and reduced the 0-62.5mph time to 7.9 seconds.

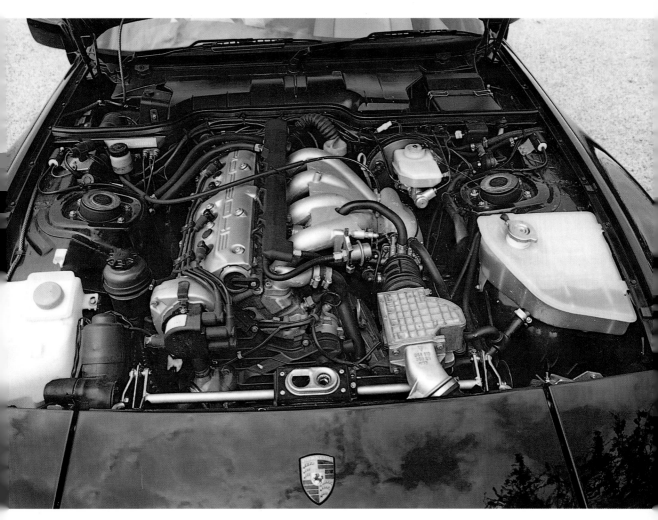

Porsche Passion

Concours — Collectables — Clubs — Competition

Porsche Club Great Britain currently runs its annual concours in mid-July at the Three Counties Showground, Malvern, Worcestershire. There is a huge indoor arena where a total of some 75 cars line up in the hope of an award, and a 'beginners' class outside. Approximately 700 spectator cars attend, bringing in well over 2,000 people. There are trade stands — including the sponsoring main Porsche dealer, with new and used Porsches on display — and diversions for the kids.

Concours events are run along scrupulously prepared guidelines and participation involves a degree of work which many would find daunting. Some call it a labour of love, others a harmless form of insanity; either way, success is sweet. Pictured opposite are Thomas Berry's concours-winning 924 Lux, and the engine compartment of Barry Roe's class-winning 924 Carrera GT.

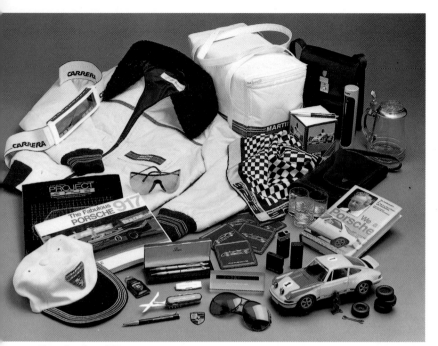

Porsche Cars GB

The acquisition of automotive literature, regalia, models and other items appeals to two categories of enthusiast (three, if you count the compulsive magpies for whom the act of collecting, rather than the objects collected, is the motivating force).

First, there are those who already own the car and wish to increase their enjoyment of it by gathering associated material; second are those for whom ownership is often an impossibility but whose fervour leads them to purchase everything which will further their knowledge or express their enthusiasm in tangible form. (These are the types who can quote entire specification sheets by heart, recite dates and chassis numbers with the ease of someone reading out a shopping-list, and remember every mistake in every book they've read. Any encounter with them demands limitless time and patience…)

Porsche enthusiasts are as susceptible as anyone else to the collecting hobby. And they are well looked after. Porsche Cars Great Britain realised very early on the marketing potential in producing good quality regalia.They call them *Porsche Possessions* and market them through their dealership network, or 'Porsche Centres' as they are designated. The range of goods available is regularly updated.

The author of this book has been collecting since 1972 and now has an impressive variety of Porsche objects — including, as pictured here on the bonnet of his 924 Carrera GT, a wide range of original factory literature. Other items range from Porsche books signed by Ferry Porsche and Derek Bell to sugar sachets from the factory restaurant in Stuttgart!

The best starting-points for collectors are specialist modelshops, bookshops (especially those dealing in secondhand literature), auto-jumbles and club magazines. There are two periodicals devoted specifically to Porsche: *911 & Porsche World* is published in the UK, and *Excellence* in California. Both carry an abundance of display and classified advertising directed at Porsche enthusiasts, as well as editorial features on Porsches past and present.

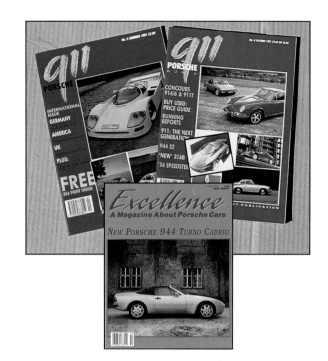

Membership of a Porsche club, whether in Britain or elsewhere, is an absolute necessity for anyone who professes an interest in the marque. Now in its 31st year and with over 10,000 members, the British Club has a thriving Motor Sport Division, an annual visit to the Stuttgart factory, concours and competition events and numerous other activities. Monthly regional meetings enable members to exchange views, and the club puts out a glossy 80-page quarterly magazine and regular listings of cars and other Porsche items for sale. The volume of Porsche know-how to be found within a club makes it a good idea to join before you buy your Porsche, rather than waiting until you have it.

Across the Atlantic, the Porsche Club of America has almost 130 regions throughout the United States and Canada. There are clubs in all major European countries, as well as in Japan, Australia, New Zealand and South Africa.

Photos Porsche Cars GB

Nearly all major manufacturers view success in motorsport as a major ingredient in the perpetual struggle to increase their market-share. German and British companies are particularly keen to attract customers by this means and one of the foremost such companies is, of course, Porsche.

To a large extent, Porsche built up its worldwide following by using the circuits to maintain a technological superiority over its rivals. Developments on the race track filter directly through to the road cars, and by winning the Le Mans 24-Hour Race more times than any other manufacturer Porsche established a name for performance and reliability which is virtually without equal.

Porsche in Germany, Porsche Cars Great Britain and most of the worldwide network of Porsche owners' clubs use motorsport to their advantage, with 924s and 944s well to the fore. As early as 1978, Porsche Cars Great Britain saw the benefits to be gained and launched an all-924 competition series. The eight rounds of racing enabled local Porsche dealers to enter the grids with well-known drivers at the wheel.

Top: The 924 gained further valuable publicity when it won the historic Commander's Cup challenge at Snetterton circuit in June 1979. The Cup is awarded to the team covering the greatest distance around the circuit in 24 hours. The two 924s ran faultlessly, clocking up over 1850 miles at an average of almost 76mph. Above: The race-bred 924 Carrera GT performed exceptionally well on its first outing at Le Mans in 1980. Porsche has had a long-standing love affair with the famous race and used it many, many times as a test-bed and proving ground. But to have all three factory-prepared cars not only finish the gruelling race but finish sixth, 12th and 13th was an achievement of high order.

The 944 also has an enviable racing pedigree. Back in 1981 a turbocharged twin-cam works special 944 (disguised as a 924 GTP) entered Le Mans to finish 7th overall and take the prize for the car having spent least time in the pits. Driven by Jürgen Barth and Walter Rohrl, it made no unscheduled stops and achieved an average speed of 114mph.

In 1986 a Porsche customer class was successfully launched with the 944 Turbo Cup race series. Further series followed, as Porsche continued to demonstrate the reliability of its cars where it really counted — on the race track — strengthening that vital relationship between competition achievement and the perceived qualities of the road cars. Porsche Club Great Britain also plays its part, its Motor Sport Division being run on a highly professional basis by club members.

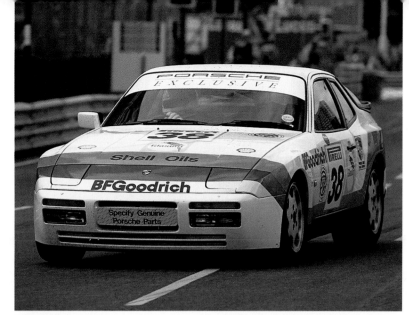

BFGoodrich

Tiff Needell in action in the 'works' 944 Turbo, which was to prove the car to beat in 1988.

Steve Kevlin's Class B, 944 S2 Cabriolet holds off Nigel Rice's tin-top 944 at Snetterton.

BFGoodrich

Enter the new: The Porsche 968

Porsche Cars GB

The new-generation 968 is more than just a 944 with a face-lift. It is an 80% new car — just as the 911 Carrera 2s and 4s were 80% new in comparison with the previous 3.2-litre Carrera models. Its styling echoes the sleek lines of the V8-engined 928, the company's flagship; especially pleasing are the 928-style pop-up headlights, Turbo-cup design wheels and 911 Turbo-type wing mirror.

Inside, the 968 varies only in a few minor details from the 944, but mechanically (as described in the specification panel) it has undergone extensive revision, with performance to match.

Porsche Cars GB

First driving reports indicate improved ride quality and reduced noise level, with overall driveability and economy adding up to what Porsche expert Michael Cotton, writing in *911 & Porsche World*, described roundly as 'a superb high-speed sports car'.

The Cabriolet, in particular, is a car which will arouse a compulsive stop-and-stare response wherever it is seen, and whatever machinery might be parked alongside it.

Porsche Cars GB
Opposite: 911 & Porsche World

PORSCHE 968 from 1991

Bodyshell:
2-door hatchback coupe and alternative Cabriolet
evolved from 944 with redesigned nose and tail.

Engine:
2,990cc 4-cylinder, developed from 944S2. Variocam
variable valve timing system. Compression ratio 11:1,
power 240bhp at 6,200rpm, torque 225lb/ft at 4,100rpm.

Transmission:
Rear-mounted 6-speed manual gearbox or 4-speed
Tiptronic dual-function automatic.

Suspension:
As 944. Spring and damper rates revised.
Height-adjustable sports suspension pack optional.

Brakes, wheels, tyres:
Ventilated discs front and rear, servo, ABS standard.
Cast light alloy 16in wheels, 7J front and 8J rear,
205/55 and 225/50 ZR16 tyres. 17in wheels, 225/45
and 255/50 ZR17 tyres optional.

Dimensions:
As 944.

Performance:
Manual; 0 to 60mph 6.5 seconds, maximum 156mph.
Tiptronic; 0 to 60mph 7.9 seconds, maximum 153mph.

Estimated price at launch:
UK £40,000,
rising to £46,000 for Cabriolet Tiptronic.

Nigel Edwards *began his writing career in 1972 with a regular motoring column for his employer's international quarterly magazine. This led to requests for other articles from local publications and to talks on car testing at motor clubs and business dinners. He now contributes regularly to the quarterly* 911 & Porsche World *and to Porsche Post.*
He is Co-chairman of the Porsche Club Great Britain Concours, having previously won the club's 25th anniversary concours with his 911SC. He was a concours judge before taking over the running of the event in 1989.
Among the 60 cars he has owned are 11 Porsches: six 911s, a 912, a 924, a 924S, a 944 and currently the 924 Carrera GT featured in this book. He is a member of both the Institute of Advanced Motorists and the exclusive High Performance Club.
In addition to his 924 Carrera GT, he currently owns an Historic Rallies Mini-Cooper S, a totally original 1968 MGB GT, a 1972 Land-Rover, a 25,000-mile 1959 Frogeye Sprite and a 1965 Royal Enfield GT Continental motorcycle.
He lives with his wife and daughter, and among a very wide variety of animals, in a Somerset farmhouse.

Simon Painter, *who took most of the pictures for this book, developed his hobby of wildlife photography into a profession on leaving school. A confirmed car enthusiast, he first ventured into automotive photography when asked to take the official photographs of the Porsche Club Great Britain National Concours in 1990. When time permits, he plays rugby for Bristol. He lives in a converted barn in Blackford, Somerset, complete with highly-equipped darkroom.*